Writing the Killer Mystery

Volume Three

Plotting the Murder

A Strategy to Develop the
Storyline of Your Mystery Novel

by

Ron D. Voigts

Ron D. Voigts

Writing the Killer Mystery, Plotting the Murder

Copyright © 2018 by Ron D. Voigts

All material and information in this book are considered factual and accurate to the author's and publisher's knowledge.

Paperback edition: October 2018, Night Wings Publishing

ISBN: 978-1726708517

Ron D. Voigts

Dedication

To my wife, Lois,

who has stuck with me and understood me

even when nobody else does

Ron D. Voigts

Books by Ron D. Voigts

Self-Published

Penelope and The Birthday Curse

Penelope and The Ghost's Treasure

Penelope and The Movie Star

Penelope and The Christmas Spirit

Claws of the Griffin

Night Wings Publishing

Strigoi, The Blood Bond

Champagne Book Group

The Witch's Daughter

The Fortune Teller's Secret

Writing the Killer Mystery

Volume One, Great Beginnings

Volume Two, Captivating Characters

Volume Three, Plotting the Murder

Ron D. Voigts

TABLE OF CONTENTS

CHAPTER SEVEN: CREATING AN EVENT-DRIVEN MURDER MYSTERY 55

CHAPTER EIGHT: LAST THOUGHTS 65

Chapter One:
Front End Stuff

First things first, I don't like reading forwards, prologues, and front end matter. Get me to the good stuff. However, I have a philosophy behind this book, the series, in fact. So stop back later if you wish to jump ahead.

I planned a five-volume series on Writing the Killer Mystery with some goals.

- Ideally, from beginning to end, these five volumes should give an excellent working knowledge of writing a mystery. Articles appear under broader headings and can be read in series-order to gain better insight into an aspect of mystery writing.

- The series is not just to inform but to inspire. Need help in finding a motive, examine the list in that section. Trying to come up with something on your sleuth's background, a list of ideas is available for your perusal. If you're stumped how to create a supervillain, a list exists for that too. Remember, these suggestions are the beginnings to stimulate your imagination. You are the author of your mystery.

- I have another philosophy. My time to read, write, handle social media, keep up with current events, take time for entertainment, and have a social life pretty much keeps me busy from dawn to bedtime, so finding moments to get absorbed in a book are hard. So, I wrote this volume in bite-size chunks to be read in short sittings. Key points, bullets, numberings, and lists are used where possible to make things easier. Examples happen at the end of many sections if more understanding is needed. The whole point is to get information fast and easy.

- The articles can stand-alone too. If you are struggling to name your sleuth, stop by that section in Volume Two for inspiration. Read the article on guns in Volume Four if you need some background. By the way, I wrote this for writers. If you check out the gun section to learn how to field strip a Glock and reassemble it, you are looking in the wrong place. Articles for nearly every facet of mystery writing can be found in the five volumes.

Following is a brief summary of contents of this third volume in Writing the Killer Mystery.

- The Fundamentals of a Plot

- The Opening Gambit

- The Middle Game

- The Big Ending

- Writing Scenes

- Creating an Event-Driven Murder Mystery

The ultimate goal of Volume Three is to build strategies for Plotting the Murder in the mystery novel.

Chapter Two:
Fundamentals of a Plot

Plotter vs. Panster

Which one are you?

The Good

Plotter = plot driven. Writing from an outline. Planning the novel's storyline. Writer's block becomes less of a problem as the narrative has been determined from beginning to end.

Panster = character driven. Developing a story moving characters toward a fuzzy ending. The plot is adjusted as the story develops.

The Bad

Plotter = a story that feels stiff and contrived. Characters seem shallow, more like actors following a script.

Panster = a story that meanders and has no direction. Writer's block is more common. Abandoned projects happen often.

Plotter Writers

J.K. Rowling

John Grisham

Panster Writers

Margaret Atwood

Stephen King

Writing a mystery book or any novel for that matter is like taking a road trip. You got the tank gassed up, a grocery bag of your favorite snacks, and a heart filled with excitement. How do you get there? You have a detailed roadmap with gas-up points, restaurants, and scenic stops. Motel reservations have been made. You have planned an arrival date and the number of miles a day. This can only be a plotter.

Or do you take off driving, knowing I95 will get you there? Your gas tank isn't full but there should be a station along the way, and they'll have snacks to buy. Should be some motels around when you need them. Your arrival will be within a few days of the target. No worry about the number of miles per day, you'll get there eventually. Yep, sounds like a panster.

Three Act Structure

Three Act Structures is probably the most popular format for writing a novel or play. When used in a drama, it is well defined and clearly laid out in the performance's program. In a book, it is less apparent but just as prevalent.

Following are the goals for each act in a murder mystery

Act I

- The opening
- The victim and crime are introduced
- The sleuth meets the suspects (including the killer) and other main characters

Act II

- The sleuth investigates the crime

- Complications arise

- Major twists happen

- The sleuths assumptions and plan fall apart

- Subplots, B-plot

Act III

- Sleuth rallies and develops a new plan

- Dramatic ending

- The sleuth reveals the killer

- Tidy up loose ends

The point here is not to learn how to write a three-act novel but to structure it using the method. The actual acts can be disregarded, but the targets in each section should be considered. When translated into a story, the distinction between acts may not be clear and don't need to be.

When taking into account each act's size or contribution to the mystery novel, the breakdown is as follows. (These are rough estimates.)

Act I = 35%

Act II = 50%

Act III = 15%

Plot Ups and Downs

The three acts are fraught with rising tension followed by brief interludes of relief. Think of tension rising in the first act followed by a moment of relief, only to experience another bought of tension exceeding the first. The pattern of tension-relief continues through the three acts until the tension reaches its maximum, otherwise known as the climax. Following it, the greatest relief comes returning things to a status quo, similar to what might have been before everything started.

Tension = creating emotion in the reader of anxiety, stress, fear, and worry

It evokes our primal emotion of fight or flight. It is the moment in the story when we want to scream "get out" or hope someone doesn't go into the basement or cringe when a man in a ski mask pulls out a machete.

Elements of Tension
Conflict
Uncertainty
Threat
Danger
Unrequited love
Revenge
Disagreements
Fear of the unknown

Tension Example

Act I

The detective comes back to the office and finds it ransacked. The intruder is hiding. They scuffle. A gun goes off.

Tension = Intruder, scuffle, the sleuth may be shot.

This is otherwise known as a cliffhanger. Note that relief comes in Act II.

Act II

The detective survives the shooting from the first act, but the intruder gets away.

Relief = Detective survives.

Later his star witness vanishes. He follows leads and finds the kidnappers hideout. Only, they are gone, and she is dead.

Tension = Witness vanishes.

Relief = Kidnappers escape and witness is dead.

Take note, the relief is not always good or positive. Only, it has eliminated the tension.

Act III

A clue leads the detective to a warehouse on the docks. He believes he has trapped the killer, but then the tables are turned. He finds himself tied up with a ticking bomb next to him. The killer explains how he is going to leave the sleuth to die and then . . .

Tension = the detective's darkest hour. He may die if he cannot escape the dilemma.

Relief = what happens next.

In novels, tension pulls us in and drives us to turn the page. In the world of TV, it takes us to the edges of our seats and the next commercial only to discover things are resolved until another advertisement comes along. The mystery writer's goal is to manipulate the tension and keep readers engaged.

How to increase tension

- Raise the stakes

- Make it personal

- Be unpredictable

- Let the killer do his or her worse

- Pile on the problems

- Create impossible challenges and setbacks

- Apply pressure

Subplots, B-Plot

In the real world, lives are complicated and have depth. We don't move linearly with only a single goal. People have multiple objectives and do myriad things. The same is true in our books.

The murder mystery has an objective: discover who killed the victim. The sleuth moves along gathering clues and overcoming obstacles. Adding subplots to the mystery creates a story rich in detail, adding complexity and depth.

Subplots interact with the main plot and the characters. It offers a diversion at times and may change the story's direction.

Romance

Everyone needs a little love. Rocky relationships attract readers. Throw someone into your sleuth's life. Love lost. Love gained.

Parallel Plot

The subplot mirrors or pivots off the main plot in some aspect and does not necessarily need to be a murder. Let's say the murder victim rescued dogs and left three behind without a home. The sleuth takes upon herself to find them homes while searching for the killer.

Character Arc

The subplot chronicles the sleuth's life and how it changes over time. This works exceptionally well in a series, spanning from book to book. This can also cover other characters in the story.

Addictions, Personal Problems

Though a bit of cliché, many murder mysteries have an alcoholic detective. Could be drug addiction. Gambling. Sexual identity. Coping with a lost love, divorce, or death. These issues not only apply to the sleuth but other characters as well. In my own book, The Witch's Daughter, Cavendish Brown struggles with his wife's death.

Dreams, Goals

Everyone has a dream, something beyond their daily routine. I worked as an engineer dreaming someday I'd be a writer. My friend hoped to someday quit his day job and get a hot dog stand. Maybe your sleuth is saving money to buy a little shack on a beach in Tahiti.

The B-Plot

This is common in screenplays. Typically a strong subplot becomes a second plot to the main storyline. Screenwriters sometimes call these the "A" story and the "B" story. The "B" story should tie in with the main plot and support it.

In my novel, The Witch's Daughter, the main plot has Cavendish struggling to find the killer of a gangster's ex-wife and locate his missing daughter. In the B-plot, Cavendish's old girlfriend arrives with over a million dollars stolen from the same gangster. The story continues between the two plots as they intersect Cavendish's life and make it difficult.

The Panster Guide to Plotting

If you are a panster, you are going to focus more on the characters and initial idea. Many authors insist their characters take over and seem to have a mind of their own. It's okay to go with the flow but be ready to do some significant editing later with perhaps lopping away stuff which doesn't work.

Here is a method I have used, and you might try. Later I will introduce a more formal approach to plotting.

ACT I

Write the first 50 pages or so to get a feel for where things are going. Get to the part where someone has been murdered. The main characters should be introduced, especially the suspects, and of course the killer.

ACT III

(Note the shift here from the first act to the third.)

Step back and review everything. Sometimes the killer is known from the beginning, and other times some re-evaluation is needed. Maybe the first choice is not the best one. The point is to stay fluid and go with what seems right. It will make for a storyline that appears not contrived.

Next, come up with the end. Not just the reveal, but the big dramatic ending. The moment pits the killer against the sleuth to see who will survive. In my own writing, I have blown up things and burnt them to the ground in the endings of my books. Write the final chapters, especially to flesh out where this is going. Remember tidying up loose ends can come later.

ACT II

Now comes the middle. List the events, the things which must happen to get from Act I to Act III. This includes finding clues, accomplishing necessary details, and putting in roadblocks to keep it from being too easy for your sleuth. More about this later.

Events will take place in the three acts, so do not think of this as happening only here. But events drives Act II. This is the place to really brainstorm ideas.

At the end of Act II, the sleuth discovers his plan, his beliefs, his theories fall apart. In my novels, I build a case pointing to someone as the murderer. The sleuth believes he has him now, but it falls apart when something shows he has the wrong person. In your work, it may mean a vital incident negating everything the sleuth has worked for.

Subplots can be introduced to create a new directions for your characters. Maybe the star witness is having an affair that may discredit her testimony. A character vanishes only to later be found having eloped with her boyfriend. The sleuth's wife's drug problem lands her in the hospital, and when he goes to be at her side, a significant clue is missed.

Act II Stall Out

Act II can be the hardest. This is where many writers fail, and writer's block sets in. Act I starts off with a bang, ACT III is planned, but Act II is a struggle. Here are some suggestions to get things rolling.

Complicate Things

This one works well when you've painted yourself into a corner and don't know how to get out. Say your sleuth is bound and sitting next to a time-bomb. He can't get loose. What do you do? Suddenly a mysterious woman comes through a window, cuts the ropes, and says,

"We got to get out of here." Who is she? That's for you to discover. Whatever you do, make sure it's an unexpected new direction.

Three Roadblocks, Three Clues

Your sleuth will need clues to guide him or her to the killer's identity. Along the way, things will happen to slow or stop progress. Remember this has to be two steps forward and one back. Even though the reader gets the feeling things aren't going well, the sleuth must pull it together in the final Act. At a minimum find three good clues and three roadblocks to progress. List them out. Work them into the storyline.

Blow It Up

This is a subset of complicate things. When you stall out in Act II, do something dramatic. An explosion works nicely, but it can be something else. A fire perhaps. Some cataclysmic event. Remember you want to rock your reader's foundation.

A Rescue

In one of my earlier mysteries, the sleuth's adopted son is kidnapped by the bad guy, and he must rescue the kid. Perhaps, in your tale, the killer snatches the detective's girlfriend and demands some item of evidence in exchange for her safe release. Some twists can be added, and of course, the daring rescue shows the sleuth's mettle.

Major Set Back

As if things could not get worse, the sleuth has a significant setback. The detective finds himself suspended after harassing a suspect; does he quit? Heck no! The private eye finds his client dead. Does she go on? The cozy sleuth discovers his house on fire destroying most everything he owns. Whatever the adversity, make it harder for the sleuth to proceed. Then let him overcome the odds.

Somebody New

A character addition can create new and unusual complications. Perhaps a mysterious person starts following the sleuth. Maybe, the murder victim's sister arrives to put her brother's affairs in order and becomes a love interest for the sleuth. In one of my novels, I had alluded to a money laundering operation, then thought why not bring in the big guy. I tweaked Act I, adding some scenes. Soon I had this powerful, ruthless gangster type trying to recoup his stolen money.

Think like the Killer

Many times mystery writers lose sight that the murderer is not going to sit by idly and wait to be caught. The bad guy or gal is going to do whatever it takes to prevent getting caught. This is a great time to put on the "evil" hat and start thinking like the killer. Remember, this is a mystery so don't tip your hat too soon about who did it.

These are a few ideas to keep things moving. Going through the list, it becomes evident these overlap and may be similar.

Act II Stall Out Fix ➜ *Complicate things!*

Timelines, The Sequence of Life

Events in the real world happen in determined order.

In the murder mystery, a crime happens, someone is murdered. Police are called. A detective emerges. Suspects are identified. Clues are found. Deductions, reason, investigation identifies the killer. The murderer is revealed. All this occurs in a timed order manner.

Whether planned or not, timelines occur in books and in real crimes. Detective investigations create timelines. Prosecutors at trials present them. Even criminals make schedules as they plan their deeds.

Timelines Resolve Things

- Establishes time-sequence of events, explaining the proper order of scenes.

- Makes clearer story timing, preventing impossibilities. An example would be a character appearing in two places at the same time. Another would be the character moving from point "a" to point "b," an impossible distance in a short time.

- Easier to follow character development through the story.

- Becomes an ad hoc storyline for those who wish to plot.

- Tracks seasons, dates, days, weeks, weather, and so forth.

Four elements recommended for the timeline

Location
Time
POV (point-of-view) Character
Scene Description

(Note: later we will revisit these when talking about scene development)

Tracking time can be vague or specific or different.
June 2, 1945, Saturday, 3:15 p.m.
Early October, afternoon.
1953
Two years ago
Yesterday
In the third millennium

For those who are following my "panster guide for plotting," I suggest adding a time stamp to each scene's beginning to keep the timeline upfront. While it does not help with seeing the big picture, it does make following the sequence of events easier.

Ron D. Voigts

Chapter Three:
The Opening Gambit

The Opening Line, Making First Impressions

Back in the day of brick and mortar bookstores, people walked the aisles, searched the bookshelves, and eyed the titles. If something sounded interesting, they'd check it out. If the cover appealed to them, they'd crack the book and read the first line. This was the make or break moment.

Today, bookstores exist, but most are online. Yet, the search continues much the same way. Title...cover...first line. If the book doesn't grab readers, they move on to the next.

The debate in writing fiction has been whether it's craft or art. The craft side will argue studying fiction, learning the profession, and applying techniques produce great works. The art side claims it's a creative process coming from the heart and soul. The reality is both are probably true.

Yet, the first line in a story comes closer to art. No magical formula will generate the words. Many variables have gone into the realm of literature past and present that has drawn readers into fictional works. Like a beautiful painting or impressive sculpture, they stand back and say, "This is art."

The first words in a book must take the reader into the work, opening doors, creating desire, wanting to know more. The first line creates questions and puzzlement, a need to go on to the next and the next. It becomes the key to imagination and the ticket to a fantastic adventure.

In a few words, the opening line grabs the reader. It conveys the author's voice. The desire to read on is spurred.

When it comes to opening lines: chose the words wisely.

Types of Opening Lines

The opening captures the reader's attention by creating questions which need to be answered. She advances through the first line, the first paragraph, the first scene. The words answer questions as new ones develop. A dance of revealing something and crafting more unknowns happens. The ultimate goal being who killed poor Mr. Victim.

Following are opening types with a few examples.

Statement

This opening type can take many variations. The main idea is to capture the reader's attention with an upfront, flat out statement. It can be dramatic, factual, set a mood or time, be surprising, or informative.

Agnes liked her men tall, handsome, and eager.

Some think Bronson is a great place to live, but its residents know otherwise.

The family pictures flying off the walls was the first sign the house was haunted.

Dramatic/Action

Plunk the reader directly into the story. No build up or explanations needed. Things are underway and rolling. Sometimes called in media res, the opening starts in the middle of the action, no flashbacks, no dialog, no explanations. Think of a movie's first scene with conflict beginning at the exciting part.

Mick slipped the revolver from his pocket, knocked on the door, and hoped no one was home.

Mr. Tims led the scalawag by his ear down the hallway to the principal's office.

I gripped the steering wheel, white-knuckled, and prayed I'd make it in time. (Openings can fit into other categories. This one works as a statement too.)

Dialog

Talk can pull the reader into the story. Some advice says not to start a story in a conversation, but if it's good go with it.

"Another dead body, just what I need."

"My mother doesn't understand me," Malcolm said and dropped a shovel full of dirt onto the body in the hole.

"The killer obviously knew what he was doing."

Description

This one can be tricky. It has to be good and done well. A reader will not settle for an opening with exposition about an image or picture. The description must be exciting and dynamic. Executed correctly, it can grab your reader and hold his attention.

The room held a peculiar scent, something from Jane's past, an odor reminiscent of cinnamon and cloves mingled with baked cookies.

The weather had been pleasant and mild, but now the air crackled with electric as thunder shook the house.

Cracked foundation, glass broken in the windows, brickwork stained from pollution and smoke, Hull House stood on the corner of North and Main like a relic from a forgotten era.

Interesting Character

A good character description will intrigue the reader and draw her into the story. The trick is to write something vibrant and captivating.

Marvin Cox kept his chin up and shoulders back as he strutted down the aisle of the church, looking more like a general than a minister.

Being a bit tall for a nine-year-old, Danny stooped forward so as not to intimidate the other boys.

Hands crippled with arthritis, shoulders stooped, and back hunched, Hazel hobbled along the street hoping to find someplace to sleep for the night.

Opening Scene

If the opening line grabs the reader, then the opening scene holds his or her attention. This is the first chance and the most likely place to lose the reader. Not finding anything exciting guarantees he or she will move on to another book.

In the classic novel, opening with the protagonist is most common. This gives the reader a chance to immediately bond with him or her. The story problem may be introduced or at least hinted about. Or the story's theme may be the focus. Perhaps the moment only serves to add the main character, anchoring his or her personality.

The murder mystery offers a different approach where the crime may be the first thing provided the reader. Often this happens in a police procedural where the misdeed occurs first, and then the detective is called in. In the cozy, the victim may be introduced with the potential suspects' interactions setting motives for the murder.

Other openings are possible but must be done well and draw the reader in immediately. If not captivating or compelling, the opening will fail.

Opening Scene Do's

1. Introduce the sleuth

2. Introduce the Crime

3. Start with the unexpected

4. Something ambiguous

5. Keep it interesting

6. Start with action

7. Conflict is a must

8. Begin in media res

Opening Scene Don'ts

1. Start with a dream

2. Begin with the weather

3. Open with backstory

4. Talk about scenery

5. Start with dialog unless its good

6. Explain things

Introducing the Sleuth

The sleuth should be introduced early in the novel. Readers identify better with him if he is brought into the mix first thing. This is not hard to do with a single point of view, and it is his. Multiple POVs make it easier to delay his introduction. Just do not wait too long.

When writing a cozy, since the murder happens off stage, this is not hard. The sleuth appears in the first scene and soon becomes involved with the investigation. In the police procedural, the crime may come first, raising the task at hand, but the sleuth must appear soon after. Delay too long, introduce too many other characters, the reader may have a more difficult time bonding with the sleuth.

Three methods for Introducing the Sleuth

- **Action**. Throw the reader directly into the sleuth's life. If she's a police detective, she slams some bad guy to the ground and cuffs them. In the cozy, the retired doctor gets word someone found her best friend dead, apparently a home invasion victim. For the private eye, perhaps the tall man wearing too much aftershave wants to hire her to follow a wayward wife. The goal is getting things moving at the start and throw the sleuth into the thick of it.

- **Dialog**. Depending on the sleuth, this can work too. Much of how he speaks can reveal himself. For the private eye, a snappy exchange of words can endear the audience to him. Perhaps the sleuth teaches at the local college and is giving a lecture on some past criminal. Or maybe he is going quip for quip with an ex-spouse. Keep in mind this is the moment that makes a lasting impression. Make sure the sleuth puts his best foot forward, so to speak.

- **Description**. This can pull the reader in with well-chosen words and an interesting character. Keep it dynamic. A grocery list of the sleuth's characteristics won't cut it. This needs to grab readers and hold their attention.

Begin with small things when introducing the sleuth. Name. Age. Gender. Description. Just a bit of the character works nicely. Something that defines him or her. But keep it simple and straightforward. This is not the time to go off on him or her, but instead, the focus needs to be on the crime to solve.

Opening chapters are not the place to bring in his or her history. That comes later. Instead, drop tidbits of information as the story progresses. Early, we learn he is separated from his wife. By chapter 5, it becomes clear he had a drinking problem and was cheating on her. A few scenes later, he regrets what happened and breaks off his affair. By mid-book, he runs into his ex-girlfriend who wants to get back together, but he blows her off. Later he tries to reunite with his wife, but she refuses. Some more backstory follows and near the book's end she serves him divorce papers. Now we have a complete picture of why he is moody and drinks too much. This is done with a sentence or two along the way and maybe a few brief scenes. The reader is not bogged down with a massive information dump. Plus this gives time for the sleuth to earn some sympathy as he regrets what he has done.

One side note mentioned in Volume 2 of this series bears mentioning here again. The sleuth must have a good reason for solving the murder. A police detective would have an apparent reason—it's his job. The private investigator may have been hired. The sleuth in a cozy may need a bit more motivation like a friend was murdered, or his help is requested. Ratcheting up things as the story continues will not hurt. The police detective discovers a cover-up within the department. The PI falls in love with her client and later witnesses him brutally killed by the bad guy. The cozy sleuth finds himself in jeopardy and possibly the next victim. The point here is giving the sleuth a reason to solve the murder and make it personal.

Introduce the Victim/Crime (You Need to Kill Someone ASAP)

The crime is the center of the murder mystery; it's the story problem. The goal from start to finish is to discover who killed the victim. Ironically, the victim, an essential character, may already be dead in the beginning.

The three primary subgenres of the murder mystery are the police procedural, the private investigator, and the cozy. The other subgenres actually derive from these. In each one, the victim/crime has a unique position.

In the police procedural, the victim/crime most resembles the stuff in the news. An apartment super finds a dead drug dealer in his building. A home invasion leaves an elderly couple dead. Two armed men take down a bank, killing a teller and guard. Construction workers find a body buried in a wall at a demolition site. A detective from the local PD is assigned to the case and must discover who did it.

The private investigator gets her work from clients who hire her to do some investigation. Though it can be to solve a murder case, typically the police are busy working that. PIs often become involved in things like blackmail, fraud, wayward spouses, surveillance, and investigations. Much of the work can come from attorneys on criminal and civil cases. During her work, a murder happens to complicate things and requiring the PI to discover who did it. The exception to letting the police find the killer is when the client feels not enough is being done and hires the PI to do it right.

For the cozy sleuth, some personal connection pulls her into the investigation. The murder victim can be a friend, a friend's friend, from her social circles, a work associate, a neighbor, an acquaintance, and so forth. Someone may request the cozy sleuth's help, knowing her reputation at solving crimes. Proximity to the murder, being in the right place at the right time, may draw her in. Unlike the first two types of crime solvers, in the cozy, the sleuth does not do this for pay and reward. Yep! It's all for duty and honor.

Presenting the crime depends on the setup. For the police procedural, it can happen as soon as the first scene. This can work for the cozy although the crime happens offstage, so opening with the sleuth pulled into solving the murder is a possibility. For the PI, some setup scenes may be necessary to get to the dead body. Ultimately, everything is based on factors in the storyline like the victim, the motive, the killer, the subgenre, and so forth.

No matter what the sub-genre type and the victim/crime, the murder needs to happen as soon as possible. Don't wait too long. The audience wants to read a murder mystery, so someone should die early in the story.

When does the murder happen?

Writers vary on how soon it occurs. Some feel within the first 10 pages, others the first chapter. Maybe the first three chapters. Or by the book's middle. Everyone has an opinion, but the murder must happen early.

Remember, wait too long and risk losing the audience.

Present the Suspects

In basic story theory, Act I has the protagonist meet the other characters. In the murder mystery, this is also true, but the focus will be on the sleuth encountering the suspects. The primary goal is getting the characters out there. Also, important to remember in the beginning, the killer is a suspect.

The suspect pool will come from two possible sources. The first type is established immediately and comes from a closed, controlled group. The suspects have been isolated from the general population. Even if not physically separated, some barrier exists. This allows the sleuth to create a suspect list to focus the investigation. This is not to say a new suspect cannot be added later, but he will somehow connect back to the original pool. This type of suspect list works well in the cozy mystery.

Cozy Suspect Pool Sources
Party
Yacht or boat
Small island
Private or boarding school
College friends
Military group
Small business or store
Close group of friends
Aboard a train or plane

The other type is an open suspect list. Here the sleuth starts with no or few suspects and gains new ones from information gathered during the investigation. This works like dominoes toppling over where one leads to the next and the next. Police procedural or private eye mysteries often take this approach where the sleuth gets a tip from a witness that leads to a suspect. Investigating provides clues which ferret out another potential suspect. More poking around, more interviewing, the suspect pool grows.

Keep in mind these two suspect groups can work across the board for different mystery types. The domino effect of finding suspects can work in a cozy, and the police procedural may draw from a closed suspect pool.

How the suspects are handled by the sleuth can vary. With the Suspect Pool, he may have an obvious task to put the puzzle pieces together. Often an evidence board is used with suspect pictures and names. Clues and notes can also be placed here. This is something seen in police work but can be used by the cozy sleuth too.

The other approach is the sleuth focusing attention on a particular suspect based on the evidence. Then she may go off on another suspect when some new clue is found. This approach may appear more convoluted and like finding puzzle pieces and assembling them on the fly.

In either case, the sleuth needs to meet the suspects in the first act of the murder mystery. Even if the suspect is not indeed a suspect at the time, contact should happen. This keeps from unexpectedly introducing a suspect later. Remember: play fair. Don't blindside the reader with a surprise suspect late in the story.

A word on introducing suspects and other players: do it slowly. A character or two per chapter works well; possibly three, but no more. Create names which do not confuse the readers with similar sound or spelling. You don't want to lose the audience early, or they may switch books and read something else.

For more information on characters, check Volume 2: *Writing the Killer Mystery, Captivating Characters*.

Chapter Four:
The Middle Game

The Sleuth Investigates the Crimes

This is where the real work begins. The sleuth has to roll up her sleeves and get cracking. Up to now, she has been getting acquainted with the crime and its elements, establishing some suspects and witnesses, and formulating an approach.

Suspects and witnesses are an excellent place to start. The sleuth will interview them, getting new insights and eliminating possibilities. Good interviewers will avoid leading questions. Yes/no responses do not gain much information. Keep things open-ended.

Leading: *Did you see Mr. Black leaving the crime scene?*

Better: *Who did you see leaving the crime scene?*

Yes/no: *Have you worked here a long time?*

Better: *How long have you worked here?*

Open-ended: *How did you meet Mr. Body?*

Good interviewing is an art. The less it sounds like a Q and A session better. Colombo in the TV series by the same name could get away with it, but you might consider a less intrusive approach. Make some small talk. Plan other things to happen in the scene.

Example: the sleuth questions the bartender at a local dive. Midway through, the owner shows up, some threats are exchanged, and the sleuth gets bopped in the eye. He leaves without getting the answers he'd wanted. And now he must develop a new approach to get the information. Plus he'll be nursing a sore eye and possibly a damaged ego.

Remember the 5 W's and an H news reporters use? Who? What? Where? When? Why? How?

For the sleuth, four are most important in solving the crime. How? Why? When? These three things must be established to show guilt. This leads to the biggie—Who?

Some Interview Questions

Where were you when the murder took place?
Who can confirm your alibi?
Who did you see leaving the crime scene?
How do you know Mr. Body?
Why did you and Mr. Body not get along?
Did Ms. Suspect did it?
Why would Ms. Suspect kill Mr. Body?
When did you hear the gunshots?
How did Mr. Body die?

One thing to remember is witnesses and suspects can lie and probably do. They have their own agendas and secrets to hide. They may protect themselves or someone else. Being forthcoming with information is not for everyone and suspicion is the name of the game. The sleuth may not trust the witness or suspect, and the reverse is also true.

Observation is another key to good sleuthing. How does the witness or suspect act when questioned or when watched? Is he or she suspicious? Does the sleuth follow him or her and discover something important? Is he or she lying? The sleuth will use her senses to gather information including sight, sound, taste, touch, and smell. Things like cameras, electronic eavesdropping, experts, and computer research come into play. The sleuth may pretend to be someone or something she is not.

The sleuth is also going to gather evidence. This might mean poking around the murder scene, sneaking into places, and being gutsy. In the police procedural, forensic evidence may also be used. Documents, objects, clues such as fingerprints and footprints, pictures and recordings are things the sleuth collects.

Some of the evidence and interview questions will lead to dead ends. But new information may be discovered. The sleuth is on a fact-finding mission, looking for the jigsaw puzzle pieces to complete the picture of how, why, and when Mr. Body was killed. Not all the pieces will fit together at first, but perseverance is the name of this game.

This whole effort is to lead the sleuth to who killed Mr. Body.

Complications

The sleuth is cranking now. Getting evidence, interviewing witnesses and suspects, the investigation is going well. She has a good idea who did it. Now comes the big reveal. Tell the world who did it! Right?

No. First, it is boring. People won't stay long with a story that goes from point "a" to "b" in a straight line. It's no fun.

Readers need excitement. They need to sit on the edge of their seats when reading the story and get their hopes up. They root for the sleuth, celebrating his successes and bemoaning the failures. This pattern continues with each goal becoming more and more difficult.

This is a roller coaster ride. We love to ride to the top and plunge down, only to head back up. We scream and shriek and applaud.

Life is not a straight line. Things come our way. We make headway. We have setbacks. It becomes an up and down battle. We hold our breath and pray we make it.

Complications will happen along the way. No such thing as a free ride. The sleuth will struggle to reach some intermediary goal. Tension will rise as we hold our breaths hoping she will make it. Success comes and the rising tension falls. Failure too can follow rising tension.

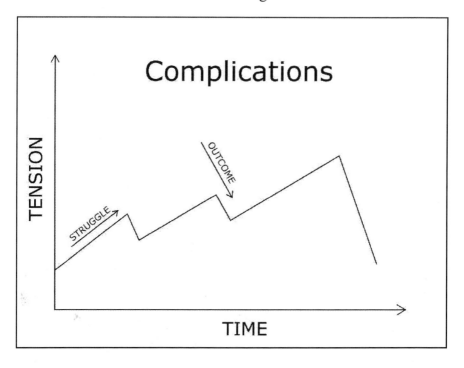

This is the stuff that makes Act II a success for the reader.

The sleuth gathers evidence and talks to witnesses and suspects. The writer of the story, therefore, needs to assign goals, a list of things that will point to a suspect as the killer. The goals are the author's devices; the sleuth may or may not be aware of the target or believe perhaps she seeks something else. When achieved, the sleuth will revel in her success; when failed, she will rally and go to the next goal.

Example

Crime: Reggie Wilson is found dead in his office, shot after work hours. Detective Mark Bracer investigates. He learns two office workers worked late and both said Reggie was in his office with someone, but they don't know who. There was shouting. The employees left soon after, but a security camera captured some details but not inside his office. Reggie watches the video. A gunshot is heard. Someone runs from the office. Another witness is spotted, coming from the women's bathroom. She and the killer run into each other. He dashes off, and she runs away.

Goal: Find the witness.

Struggle: The witness is the new accountant, Mary Stanworth. No one knew she stayed late. She doesn't come to work the next day nor answer her cell phone. Mark goes to her apartment. Her roommate says she came home from work, packed a few things, and left with no word to where. He checks with her boyfriend. The guy knocks down Mark and escapes on his motorcycle. Later, the boyfriend is arrested after a barroom fight. Mark questions him. He doesn't know where Mary went and ran when he thought Mark was going to arrest him for back parking tickets. Later her body is found in an abandoned building by teenagers smoking pot. Someone shot her and dumped the body.

Outcome: This is a negative result. Detective Mark is back to square one and must take a new approach.

The outcome can be positive. Again this is two steps forward and one back. The whole point is to create "tension." Will he succeed or won't he? We hold our breaths. We keep fingers crossed. And we keep rooting for him.

Tension is stretching a rubber band and seeing if it will break. Only this rubber band is the struggle. The outcome is sometimes negative and sometimes positive. Good moments come, and we cheer. Bad ones happen, and we gasp and cry.

Not all struggles are to solve the crime. The sleuth has demons to contend with like alcohol, drugs, and health issues. Perhaps he tries to reconcile with his wife. Maybe it's something from his past. This is where subplots come in.

Also of note, the struggles get harder, and the tension grows as the story progresses. This is an uphill battle, and only the sleuth can do it. He may not succeed at times and be close to quitting, but he doesn't. The rewards will come as he gets closer to his goal—apprehending the killer.

Major Twists

Every mystery novel needs a major twist or two or possibly three. Too many are not good, but a few can draw the reader in deeper and break up what might become a boring, predictable plot. Instead, it inserts intrigue and suspense into the story.

When introducing the plot twist, it must be a surprise. No foreshadowing aloud. Giving even the slightest hint will destroy the shock factor. Here are a few ideas.

Another Murder

This becomes the didn't-see-it-coming moment. Somebody else dies, the second victim. Maybe he knew too much. Perhaps she was blackmailing the killer. Someone close to the investigation works best. A significant murder twist that always works well is the sleuth who has become romantically involved with the witness or client, only to see her die and cannot do anything to prevent it. This will drive the sleuth even harder to find the killer. Of course in all cases, the killer continues to remain unknown.

Unexpected Character

The suspects are introduced in Act I, but an unexpected witness or essential character arrives in Act II and totally changes things. Best to use an example. The private detective is close to proving his client did not murder her husband and deserving of the inheritance. The dead man's children by a previous marriage find someone who claims to be the woman's first husband to whom she is still married and thus prove she is not reliable and undeserving and never legally married to their father. This is the moment when the detective says, "You didn't think it was important to tell me?" The unexpected character and how he or she relates to the story must be plausible.

180-Degree Turn

The sleuth has been pursuing something that can prove her case but suddenly takes an entirely different direction. An example again: she struggles to find the witness, Mr. Jones. After multiple failures, she turns to her sidekick and says, "If we can't find Mr. Jones, maybe he will have to find us," and they set a plan in motion. This type of action shows the sleuth's cleverness which takes the sidekick and reader by surprise.

Second Murder, While the Suspect is in Jail

The sleuth and everyone believe they've caught the killer. Arrests have been made. Bail withheld. It's all over everyone thinks. Then another murder happens with the same MO and is apparently related to the first murder. Back to square one!

Freak Accident and a Dead Witness

A witness is found who will prove the case against the suspect and land him in jail for a long sentence. It's a pat case. No loose ends. The witness is set to testify. On the way to the courthouse steps off the curb and is run down. She's pronounced dead on the spot. The car and driver are long gone. Like before, back to square one.

The more of an oh-my-gosh moment, the better the twist. Above all else, it needs to be a surprise. If the reader sees it coming, it's not a twist.

The Sleuth's Assumptions and Plan Fall Apart

Act II, the middle game, is fraught with struggles. At times the sleuth feels downhearted and frustrated. But progress is made, and things begin to take shape. She gathers evidence. She interviews witnesses and suspects. One suspect starts to look guilty. This is the moment she has worked for. She plans to apprehend the culprit and may even haul him off to the hoosegow.

Something goes terribly wrong. What seems obvious becomes obscure. The sleuth made a mistake because a premise was false, some evidence was not what it seemed, a witness gave an inaccurate account, something was missed, and the list goes on. The bottom line is she got the wrong man or woman.

Everything falls apart for the sleuth in Act II. The whole investigation seems to be a failure. It's back to square one again.

Let's take a look at the earlier example.

Recap: Reggie Wilson is shot, working late at his office. Two witnesses hear the gunshots but cannot identify the assailant. Another witness sees the culprit but is later found dead.

Further investigation: After a key witness is found dead, Detective Mark Bracer receives a tip that the murder weapon, a gun, is owned by Kelvin March, Reggie's former business partner. The gun is tested; rifling marks on the bullet matches the slug removed from Reggie's chest. A witness at a local bar overheard Reggie and Kelvin arguing over a venture gone sour and Kelvin threatening to kill Reggie. Further investigation found Reggie embezzled funds from their now-defunct business leaving Kelvin bankrupt.

Outcome: With high fives around the police station and much back patting, Detective Bracer heads to Kelvin's home and arrests him for murder. Later Kelvin's lawyers provide video of their client at a night baseball game during the time of the killing. A judge dismisses the charges.

Of course, much could happen here, but for the moment everything the sleuth has struggled to prove has fallen apart. Kelvin is an innocent man and cannot have killed Reggie.

Failure is the final outcome after the sleuth has gone through many struggles. The sleuth's assumptions appear flawed. The plan to arrest someone falls apart. To sum: the Sleuth has failed.

How the sleuth handles failure will vary. Perhaps binge drinking comes. Maybe a visit to an old girlfriend for solace is needed. Personally, I'd go with a large container of Rocky Road ice cream. But this must smack of failure.

☞ **Failure = not catching the bad guy**

The Deadend Dilemma

An alternate version of the "sleuth's failure" can play out. Instead of finding someone and learning it's the wrong person, the detective comes up empty-handed. He's got clues, motives, and suspects but nothing adds up. The investigation has reached a dead end.

Sulking, frustration, anger, and bewilderment are some of the sleuth's reactions. The puzzle pieces should go together but don't. The sleuth reviews the evidence to discover what has been missed. Her attitude is "the answer is here somewhere but what am I not seeing." Important to note, the sleuth has the necessary evidence but is missing a detail. The problem is discovering what it is.

☞ **Failure = not seeing the big picture**

Ron D. Voigts

Chapter Five:
The Big Ending

Sleuth Rallies and Develops a New Plan (It's always darkest before the dawn.)

At the end of Act II, the sleuth's efforts to find the killer have failed. She made assumptions based on evidence and witness accounts. Her certainty was high.

Perhaps an arrest was coming. Maybe the sleuth shared her convictions with someone. Whatever happened, her suspect was not the killer. Some new evidence came to light. His weak alibi suddenly became a pat one. Sometimes the supreme failure happens when the number one suspect becomes the next victim.

And perhaps she's hit a dead end and has nothing.

This is a devastating moment. The sleuth will rack her brain trying to find an answer. The moment is fraught with frustration. Some sleuths turn to alcohol. Others become moody. The workaholics try harder. Even the most level-headed, even-keeled sleuth will acknowledge the failure.

Something happens. Enlightenment comes. This is the light bulb moment. A clue, some words, a witness's comment come back to her. She suddenly sees it in a new light. This is the "Aha!" moment.

"Aha!" Moments

- The sidekick says something offhand and reminds the sleuth of an earlier clue, putting it into a new light.

- A parallel event gives the sleuth a new perspective on an existing clue.

- Sherlock Holmes: "Watson! I know who did it."

- The sleuth combs through the evidence looking for something missed.

- Something thought not important becomes the key to the mystery.

- A remark by a witness or suspect never considered significant becomes paramount to finding who did it.

Whatever the catalyst, the evidence has to be in plain view and available to the reader. No surprises. No pulling rabbits out of the hat. This is the fair play part where the reader has as much a chance as the sleuth in solving the crime. But the sleuth was smart, and now she knows.

Sleuth Reveals the Killer (The Big Reveal)

After the sleuth knows who did it, the Big Reveal comes. If this is done well, the reader will not yet know and anxiously await the news. Methods to reveal the killer are as numerous as the ways to kill the victim.

Big Reveal Ideas

- In the classic cozy, the sleuth will gather the suspects together and explain all. Evidence will be cited, witness details recalled, and logic revealed. One by one the suspects will be identified as to why they could have killed the victim and why they did not. This will ultimately lead to revealing the killer.

- A trap is set based on the new evidence. The killer is forced to expose himself. The moment is fraught with drama and danger.

- If a police procedural, an arrest may be imminent. Shootouts are fun. Maybe a moment of reckoning for the killer with one last plea and an attempt to escape.

- Sometimes the murderer commits suicide when confronted with his crime. Remorse over his deed, refusal to go to prison, or a drive to die seals this ending.

- The killer escapes. Always great for a sequel.

- The killer is allowed to go free. The victim committed such heinous crimes his killing seems justifiable. The sleuth looks the other way and lets the killer go. This has to be done well.

- As before, the victim committed crimes which make his killing seems justifiable. But wrong is wrong, and the sleuth does her job. The good news is the killer gets a light sentence.

The Dramatic Ending

Revealing the murderer is every mystery's goal. Discover who did it and tell the reader becomes the culmination of everything that has transpired in the novel. By its nature, the "Big Reveal" can add a dramatic note to end the story and may be enough to conclude things.

But adding some pizazz to the end can liven things up. Going out with some fireworks can leave your readers breathless. It becomes the moment when he says, "Wow! That was worth the journey."

The Dramatic Ending = Sleuth vs. Bad Guy

Seeing who will win!

Ending on a Bang!

Although not necessarily a real bang something like it never hurts. And if it is a bit spectacular, then the better. In my book The Fortune Teller's Secret, Cavendish discovers the murderer's identity and confronts him. Unfortunately, the killer decides to end his life by setting fire to the fireworks truck parked behind the carnival. Skyrockets and aerial bombs and things which sparkle launch from the truck for the next half hour decimating the carnival and put Cavendish and Alex's life in danger.

The Sleuth is Going to Die

The sleuth finds himself in the final struggle with evil and is losing. We want to see good prevail and when it doesn't, we feel helpless and devastated. The moment is fraught with despair. Imagine the sleuth locked in mortal combat with the killer and thrown off the cliff. Now Mr. Bad Guy turns to kill his last victim. If done correctly, the reader will be surprised and applaud when the sleuth miraculously comes back to save the day.

Someone Else is Going to Die

The sleuth races to find someone who may die at the hands of the killer. Perhaps the victim's whereabouts are not known. Maybe booby traps have been set to prevent a rescue. But whatever the roadblocks, the clock is ticking and things look bleak. A last minute save, just in the nick-of-time, goes over well here.

The Big Clash

This is a bunch of good guys go after the bad guy. The endings are never pretty. Lawmen ambushed Bonnie and Clyde in a spray of gunfire. Butch Cassidy and Sundance faced the Bolivian army, well at least in the movie. The S.W.A.T. team crashes in and rescues the kidnapped child and kills the bad guys.

Something Bad Will Happen

Unlike the "Big Bang" ending, this is more anticipation of a dramatic finish. The sleuth is given a choice where he can only save one person and let another die. A variation is having to rescue someone while allowing the bad guy to escape. In either case, the sleuth will need a good alternative plan the bad guy didn't see coming.

The Ending Twist

The end-of-Act I twist and mid-Act II twist have been discussed, but this one is a final surprise. It usually comes as part of the big reveal when the murderer turns out to be someone totally unexpected. The big shock comes in Agatha Christie's The Murder of Roger Ackroyd when we learn the killer is Dr. James Sheppard, the novel's narrator and least suspected person.

Someone Else Kills the Bad Guy

This one needs to be done right as the sleuth must prevail as the hero. In my book The Witch's Daughter, Cavendish is locked in mortal combat with the kidnapper, and it isn't going well. In an unexpected moment, the kidnap victim clobbers the bad guy from behind with a tire iron. The moment gives Cavendish time to get the victim away and to medical help.

Tidy Up Loose Ends

Murder mysteries have loose ends after the big reveal. These can be cumbersome and drag out the ending once the killer is known. Readers are ready to move on to the next book, so plan to wrap things up.

The best ending is a few paragraphs, maybe a page or two, after the big reveal. Then comes THE END.

Unfortunately, many writers do not plan well, and much needs to be explained. I read a murder mystery recently where the book went for 38 more pages after the killer was arrested. I found myself skimming and looking ahead.

Some Things to Try

- Resolve subplots before the big reveal.

- Write tight after the big reveal. Don't drag it out.

- A little "telling" is okay. Summarize outcomes.

- Plan ahead.

- Imply.

On this last one, in The Witch's Daughter, a character disappears, apparently drowned, no body found. I could have written a whole chapter of what happened to her. Instead, I did it directly. A postcard arrived in the sleuth's mail. A picture of a sandy beach with palm trees and a caption "Greetings from the Grand Cayman Island" adorned the front. On the back was no signature or return address. That was it. Who sent it was apparently the missing woman. Nothing more need to be said about her fate.

A word on the ending. Loose ends must be tidied up and resolved. To leave something open-ended can disappoint readers.

But what about a sequel? Leaving an open question is permissible. The suggestion is to tidy up the loose ends and then pivot off something in the story.

Example

In The Fortune Teller's Secret, the question is raised whether the main character is adopted or the biological child of his parents. His mother supplies his birth certificate, proving he is their child by birth. Ah-hah! The loose end is tidied up. In an epilogue chapter, another character finds a reference in a letter describing an infant placed in the care of people who strangely sounds like him and his parents. Is it? Come back for the next book.

Chapter Six:
Writing Scenes

Structure of a Book

To understand a scene, it needs to be shown in the context of the other elements in a book. The typical flow is as follows.

Words >>> Sentences >>> Paragraphs >>> Scenes >>> Chapters >>> Book

I have seen some novels omit an element like the chapter with one scene after another. Once or twice I've encountered a book that seems to be an information free fall with no apparent structure. When writing the mystery, most readers will expect a certain standard. Best advice is stick to what is typical.

Chapters

These represent the largest break in a book. Some writers use long chapters with many scenes, and others have shorter ones with numerous scenes in their books. They can be titled or numbered or both. Authors have different philosophies on chapter breaks. Generally, scenes in a chapter will move toward some specific goal.

Scenes

They show one or more characters involved in the action and/or dialog incorporating conflict and tension. Scenes have a beginning, a middle, and an end. They present some event or goal (even if not successful) necessary to move the story forward.

Words, sentences, and paragraphs will not be discussed here and are best left to a book on grammar.

It would be remiss to not mention a few other parts of a book not covered in a chapter or scene.

Prologue

An introduction which provides background for the story but may not be absolutely necessary to the plot. If it is required, it should probably be a chapter. Often it chronicles a past incident of a character or some event related to the novel.

Epilogue

Like the prologue, it chronicles what happens after the story has ended, covering the characters or possibly hinting at a future extension of the storyline or sequel.

Preface

An introductory essay from the author explaining the story development, significant features, and background. Often the author will make acknowledgments and credits to people and organizations helpful in developing the book.

Foreword

Written by someone else other than the author, it acts as an introduction of the work and/or the author. In chronology, the foreword comes before the preface.

What is a Scene (Making a Scene)

A scene can be short or long. It is an event needed to move the story forward. The scene can affect a character arc but contributing to the story is paramount.

Characters

The scene has one or more characters involved in some action contributing to the plot or subplot.

Point-Of-View

The point-of-view needs to be established early, typically in the first sentence or two. If the novel is a single POV, say the sleuth's, then the reader will accept the orientation. When writing with multiple POVs, the viewpoint must be established soon to avoid confusing the reader.

Location

This too must be established soon, again in the first sentence or so. Without it, the reader will feel lost and confused.

Goal

The scene has a goal or purpose. Something happens which impacts the storyline. The outcome may be a success or a failure. A success moves things forward. A failure may require another attempt, a reevaluation, or a goal's abandonment. The outcome also creates possible future goals.

Tension/Conflict

The action must escalate and pull the reader in. Will the sleuth succeed or won't he. What are the stakes? Life or death? Are we closer to solving the crime? Even a small goal needs to draw readers in and make them hold their breaths waiting for an outcome.

Beginning, Middle, End

The scene almost becomes a mini-story within the novel. It opens, something happens, and concludes. The outcome can be positive but may be negative too. The end should leave the reader hanging and wanting to read on.

Scene Example

Characters—Detective Mark Bracer, unknown driver of a black SUV.

Point-of-View—Detective Mark Bracer.

Location—Inside his car, heading home.

Goal—Escape the car following him.

Tension/conflict—Things will escalate from being followed to someone trying to kill him.

Beginning—Mark pushes the key into the car's ignition and considers for a moment if he should drive after downing three whiskey sours at his favorite bar. (This accomplished the POV and location in one swoop.) Driving home he now spots a car following. This sets the goal—lose the car following him.)

Middle—Things escalate into a high-speed chase. The car comes closer and smashes into his bumper. He spots a hand poking a gun out the driver's window, and a shot is fired. He makes a final attempt to lose the car and takes a sharp turn. An old woman steps off the curb. He swerves and rolls the car. (Tension mounts. The reader is drawn into the moment, waiting to see what happens next.

End—He awakes in his car, which now is on its side. A uniform cop is standing above him and says, "Had a few drinks tonight?" (Outcome: wrecked the car, may be in trouble, escaped with his life, and now he needs to discover who was after him and why. The question by the cop leaves the reader hanging and wondering what will happen next.)

Starting a Scene

Two things need to be established immediately in a scene opening.

- Who is the POV (point-of-view) character?

- Where is the location?

If the story is using a single POV, the reader will assume it's the same character. But even a book with a single POV needs some reassurance it is the same person as before, especially in the early chapters. In a first-person POV, using "I" in the opening is a dead giveaway. A third-person POV needs to be a bit more visible and incorporate the character's name.

A multiple POV storyline definitely needs the character's identity out there as soon as possible. Nothing can be more confusing than not knowing from whose viewpoint the scene is written. Best to work the character's name in within the first few sentences, no later than the second paragraph.

Now I am sure exceptions will arise. Consider if the reader can recognize whose POV the scene starts with. Ask someone else to read it and see if they can tell.

Location is the next must. A few words. A description. Something to clue the reader where the scene is taking place. Context may also give a hint of location.

Context Example

Martin opened a can of cat food and dumped it into Fluffy's bowl.

Now, as it stands, it would be difficult to know where this scene takes place. Does Martin work at a pet store where he feeds the cats? Maybe he's at his sister's house and taking care of her kitty while she is away. But if established early he owned a cat that lived in his apartment, the reader would infer the location as his home.

Another example of context comes when a scene is undoubtedly the continuation of an earlier scene. Again some clue is required to tie it together.

Continuation Example

The scene takes place at Matt's apartment where he and a friend, Dick, have been arguing. Here is the closing line.

Dick pulled the gun from his jacket pocket and aimed it at Matt's head. "Give me a reason not to shoot you."

The second scene opens as follows.

Matt narrowed his eyes at Dick. "I can give you a few good reasons not to pull the trigger."

From the context, we can deduce it is still Matt's apartment.

But if context does not carry it, something must cue the reader where the scene takes place.

Scene direction

Some objective should become evident. The scene cannot meander without a direction. A goal can be positive or negative, but something must happen.

The POV character may set a direct goal. The sleuth may head out to interrogate a witness. Perhaps she has a hunch where the murder weapon was hidden. Maybe a tipster wants to meet him at some sleazy out-of-the-way bar. Keep in mind a non-sleuth character can also set a goal.

But the goal can be unplanned. This happens when someone, something, or just plain bad luck set the direction. A thug waits at the sleuth's apartment, hiding in a closet, with plans to shoot him. An ex-girlfriend arrives at his apartment asking for help to escape a stalker. A woman makes a bank deposit when masked men rob the bank.

Always, the goal will have a purpose and contribute to the plot. A scene having nothing to do with the storyline should not be included. New writers have a tendency to fill the book with details of a character's life to account for his whereabouts at all times. Not necessary. Just write what is needed.

Tension builds. Attaining the goal should not be easy. Pitfalls, roadblocks, and detours will come. The POV character will push forward or try to escape. Things will be difficult.

Not every scene needs to be a life and death matter. In fact, too much tension for too long can wear out the reader. The degree of tension varies and generally escalates as the story moves forward. After intense scenes, a quieter one will follow. One scene has the sleuth trying to protect a client. The bad guys are relentless. In the end, the client dies, but somehow the sleuth survives. In the next scene, he drinks heavily hoping to forget (yep this can be a goal too!). A sympathetic friend listens and convinces him to bring the killers to justice.

Every scene has an outcome and ending which will be positive (a success) or negative (a failure).

Leave Them Wanting More (aka the cliffhanger)

Readers turn pages because they want to know what comes next. The best way to give them a reason to continue is ending chapters on cliffhangers. This works well with scenes too. Just save the best ones for chapter endings.

Know when to stop. Many writers continue to write after dumping the cliffhanger, thinking something needs further explanation. The cliffhanger primarily is designed to leave the reader in the dark in a fun way. Hence the hanging part.

The closure will be needed in the next scene, the next chapter, or perhaps a few scenes and chapters later. Don't drag it out too long. Too much anticipation for too long will eventually drive the reader off, in a search for some better entertainment.

Some Types of Cliffhangers

1. Something terrible is going to happen, aka impending danger.

Examples—

Milly slipped the gun from her purse, took aim, and pulled the trigger.

Ben froze. On the table lay the bomb, and the clock was ticking. 8. . . 7. . . 6. . .

2. Surprise. Some are good, and some are bad.

Examples—

Frank's fingers trembled as he opened the envelope and removed the letter. The signature caught his attention immediately. He recognized the name of his wife who had died seven years earlier.

Helen unwrapped the little box wondering what Art had given her. Inside she found a ring with the biggest diamond she'd ever seen.

3. The revelation or discovery.

Examples—

Philip jimmied the desk drawer lock and slid it open. Inside lay the missing pages of his father's will.

Maggie wrung her hands together and said, "Sorry, Jim, but the baby is yours."

4. Open-ended decision or consequence.

Examples—

Maggie gasped as she realized what she must do.

Only one outcome could come, and Freddy dreaded it.

5. A Problem

Examples—

Bobby stood in front of the two doors. Opening one would trigger a bomb, and the other would lead to freedom. Which one to pick?

Buddy stared at the safe. He'd cracked many in his career, but it took time. Kane's men were on their way, and he didn't have the luxury of time.

6. A Failure.

Examples—

Martha had hoped the surprise would cheer Mama up, but instead, it sent her depression into a downward spiral.

The case should have been open and shut. The witness could have put Johnny Valentine away for life. Only the witness now lay on the sidewalk with a bullet hole in her head.

7. Foreshadowing

Examples—

Roger stood near the front door, his Glock tucked in his belt. Outside the police waited for daybreak. He'd make his stand and hoped his wife would understand.

Dr. Mills nodded and agreed to perform the surgery, knowing the procedure would never succeed.

8. Open-ended dialog

Examples—

Helen grinned at Steve. "So what do we do now?"

Tom awoke to the muzzle of a Smith and Wesson aimed at his nose. Mr. Karol grinned and said, "Now, we're going to have that little talk."

9. Emotion

Examples—

Louise crushed the telegram with the news of her husband's death. How impersonal! She fell onto the bed and wept.

Fanny through her husband's clothes out onto the lawn and screamed.

10. A Secret

Examples—

Carol remove the yellowed envelope from behind the dresser drawer where she'd hidden it five years earlier. The time to tell Kenny the truth had come.

Harold lied for twenty years about what happened to his father. Now he wondered if the moment had arrived to explain everything.

This list should give some good ways to craft a cliffhanger. The more you write and incorporate these into your work, the more it will become second nature. The list is not exclusive, and you may find your own tricks. Also, you may find a cliffhanger falling into multiple categories.

Best to remember, the key to a cliffhanger is something more is to come, and the reader is left at a dramatic moment of what it is. When done well and throughout the book, readers will want to keep reading. The biggest compliment a writer can get is "I couldn't put the book down until I finished reading it."

☛ **Writing a good scene is part of the craft. Ending it is the art.**

Ron D. Voigts

Chapter Seven:
Creating an Event-Driven Murder Mystery

Key Events, Just the Main Stuff

Six key events are needed to define the mystery novel. More can exist, but these are needed. I've discussed them earlier, but here they are again, better organized. If you are a panster, these are worth noting and using. For the plotter, they are used in the next few sections. Most likely, you fall somewhere in between. Best to use these.

Opening (Act I)

Sets the pace for the story and may include the murder. Possibly this is where we meet the sleuth. What appears here sets the story in motion, sometimes called the inciting incident.

End of Act Twist (Act I)

End the first act with a major cliffhanger, a page-turner. Keeps the momentum going.

Mid-Act Twist (Act II)

Continue the momentum. Something dramatic needed here.

Assumption Failure (Act II)

Things fall apart for the sleuth. Whoever seems to be the murder is not. Or maybe after all the hard work, he's got nothing. Whichever, it's a dark moment.

Catalyst (Act III)

The sleuth has a revelation. The "Aha" moment. Something pulls it together, and now he knows who did it. Of course, the truth will be revealed later.

The Big Reveal (Act III)

This is where it happens. The sleuth lets everyone in the story and, of course, the readers know who did it.

This is the basis for Plotting the Murder. The writer's goal is to establish the key events and supply what's in between.

Read on for a method to do that.

Events Drive the Plot

Notice in the last section I subtly introduced the idea of an "event" into developing the plot. Let's get a bit deeper into the event-driven plot.

An event is something happening. It may take one scene or many ones to cover what transpires. Events chain together to form a plot. Events can happen in parallel. They can be independent and sometimes converge.

Everything starts with the "Opening" event and leads to the "Big Reveal" event, though the reality is a tidy up event is also needed. Plotting the murder mystery looks something like this.

Act I

Opening Event

More Events

End of Act Twist

Act II

More Events

Mid-Act Twist

More Events

Assumption Failure Event

Act III

Catalyst Event

More Events

Big Reveal Event

Tidy Up Event

Event Summary

- Event = something happens

- One or more scenes = an event

- A story = Once upon a time something happens and then something happens, and then something happens . . . and then something happens, and they lived happily ever after.

Documenting the Plot

Events become milestones. Plotting is not about writing scenes but determining events needed to get from the Opening to the Big Reveal. How to document the events is a matter of choice.

Note Cards

My favorite is the 4x5 index cards. The smaller cards (3x5) don't have enough room. The bigger ones (5x8) are a bit awkward to handle.

The event is written at the top. Notes can be added as needed to the card. The beautiful thing is cards can be arranged and rearranged as needed. If notes get long, two or more cards can be used and held together with a paperclip.

For organizing, use an index card box with dividers. Mark the dividers Act I, Act II, and Act III. Drop the cards into the appropriate section. If you have followed the earlier volumes in this series, dividers can be added for Mystery Novel Plan and Character Profiles.

In later examples, I will use index cards, but please adapt the following methods as needed.

Loose Leaf Paper and Binder with Dividers

The same can be done with hole-punched, loose-leaf paper, devoting a page to each event. Mark dividers as above with Act I, Act II, and Act III. Dividers can be added for Mystery Novel Plan and Character Profiles. Here a page will be devoted to the 5 Story Model Elements and to each character profile.

Scrivener

Literature and Latte makes a slick program called Scrivener which has capabilities for word processing, organizing notes like events, and much more. Folders can be added with files for Plot Events, the Mystery Novel Plan, and Character Profiles.

Other Methods

Here are some other ideas although they may not lend well to organizing and arranging as the previous methods.

- Legal pad

- Composition book

- MS Excel spreadsheet

- MS Word with Outlining

- A whiteboard and dry erase markers

The Task of Plotting

Following are the goals when plotting. Although numbered here for clarity, they need not be done in the order shown. Most times jumping around and updating earlier notes will be necessary.

1. Document Mystery Novel Plan (Writing the Killer Mystery, Volume 1)

2. Document Character Profiles (Writing the Killer Mystery, Volume 2)

3. Create the six Key Events and add to Act I, Act II, and Act III as appropriate.

4. Determine clues, evidence, milestones, complications, twists, information needed, setbacks, subplots, and whatever else may be required. This is the fundamental brainstorming part.

5. Create Events needed to move through the Acts and document on index cards, or use another method. Tuck them in the Act I, Act II, and Act III positions, roughly according to chronological order.

Sculpting the Plot

A sculpture does not start chiseling a chunk of marble on one end and work to the other. Rather he chips away here and there and steps back to look at it. He takes off more stone and evaluates. Slowly the shape of something becomes visible. More shaping and observing as details become clear.

So it is with plotting and writing. An event of finding a clue is needed between the beginning of Act II and the mid-Act twist. Create a card and tuck it into the correct location. A suspect needs to be interrogated in Act I, so another event card gets done. An idea for Act III comes, and another event card gets placed in the correct location. The process continues as more events come up and get documented.

Jumping around and filling gaps will produce an event-driven murder mystery. But can plotting be done from start to end? Absolutely. Pansters will typically start at the beginning and work to the end. But developing an event-driven outline allows working on different parts of the plot, out of order, as the muse dictates.

Also, like the sculptor refining his work, the author can expand on event notes adding details at any time. Parts grow, and the plot takes form. Many times the event cards have so much information that writing the scenes happens quickly with little or no writer's block.

More than one card may be needed. No problem. Use what is required and paperclip the cards together.

Plotting upfront cuts down writing time later.

Events and Scenes Examples

As mentioned earlier, an Event may be one or more scenes depending on how it's documented. Here is an example from an upcoming book, The Thief' Return, where an event card leads to four scenes..

Event: Jane goes to Florida with Benson Briggs. Cavendish and Alex go after her.

- Scene 1: Cavendish gets a call that Jane has vanished at her work.

- Scene 2: Alex and Cavendish go to her workplace and learn from other employees she went off with a bearded man who sounds like Benson Briggs.

- Scene 3: Marbella Wellingway, the mentor to Cavendish, tells him to go to Florida and get Jane back.

- Scene 4: Cavendish and Alex fly to Miami where Bob, a family friend, picks them. up

More Thoughts on Events

The writer controls the Event definition. In the previous example, I had written it as one event. But it could have been done as two events.

- Jane goes to Florida.

- Cavendish and Alex go after her.

The Event could have been split down further to its more basic element, the scene. Then the Events could be as follows.

- Jane vanishes.

- Briggs has taken her to Florida.

- Marbella Wellingway sends Cavendish and Alex after her.

- Cavendish and Alex arrive in Florida.

But if the original Event Card were left as a single event citing four possible scenes, no problem.

When writing from the card with multiple scenes, do them in one swoop. If another Event Card has scenes happening in parallel do them next. Later the scenes can be reordered to make more sense and preserve the correct chronology.

A second Event Card follows.

- Jane and Briggs at a hotel in Florida.

- Briggs leaves to talk to a retired detective who worked on the diamond heist.

I wrote these two Events scene by scene and then reordered everything to allow for the correct chronology of events. Here is the final scene sequence.

- Jane vanishes. (Event Card #1)

- Briggs has taken her to Florida. (Event Card #1)

- Jane and Briggs at a hotel in Florida. (Event Cart #2)

- Marbella Wellingway sends Cavendish and Alex after her. (Event Card #1)

- Briggs leaves to talk to a retired detective who worked on the diamond heist. (Event Card #2)

- Cavendish and Alex arrive in Florida. (Event Card #1)

Typically, I make my scene notes on the same Event Card even if multiple scenes are needed. Again adding a card for more details only means using a paperclip to keep things together.

☛ **Event-driven Plots = Better Perspective and Clearer Outlines**

Why Events?

An argument could be made that plotting should be nothing more than a series of scenes sequenced to create a storyline. Plotting scene by scene can be difficult. The problem is getting too close to the forest and not seeing trees. This is a strong reason why some lean toward the panster approach and avoid plotting. Too much to think about.

Another analogy is perhaps useful. Event driven plotting is like designing a wall. You don't plan to build brick by brick, just as not plotting scene by scene. Getting every brick or scene location figured out becomes tedious work. Instead a good foundation is devised, just as key events are for the plot. Details in the wall are planned like windows and doors; events for three acts are designed into the story. When the time arrives to build, bricks are laid in place and scenes are put into the novel.

If someone could create a deck of cards with all possible events, then we'd only need to select the cards for our story and lay them out on the table in correct order. The good news is we can do that. Only here we get to make up our own set of event cards.

Step back!

Take a deep breath.

Try event-driven plotting.

Ron D. Voigts

Chapter Eight:
Last Thoughts

Just a Few Words, Please

Thank you for taking the time to read *Writing the Killer Mystery: Plotting the Murder, Volume Three*. The plan presented here is a sure strategy to develop the murder mystery storyline. If I've helped and you found this useful, please let others know and leave a few words on Amazon about the book. The link below is provided for your convenience.

https://amzn.to/2KXMuws

Writing the Killer Mystery Series

Volume 1: Great Beginnings (Released April 2018)

- Mystery Writers and Their Sleuths

- Understanding the Mystery

- Types of Mystery

- Got a good idea?

Volume 2: Captivating Characters (Released May 2018)

- The Sleuth

- The Victim

- The Killer

- The Suspects

- Special Characters

- The Rest of the Characters

Volume 3: Plotting the Murder (Released July 2018)

- The Plot
- The Opening
- The Middle Game
- The End
- Scenes

Volume 4: Places, Clues, and Guilt (October 2018)

- Setting
- Means, Motive, Opportunity
- Clues, Red Herrings, Misdirection
- History, Backstory

Volume 5: Getting it Right, Getting Paid (January 2019)

- Writing Advice
- Revision
- Publishing
- Promotion

Note: release dates and content of future volumes are subject to change. Please stop my website at http://www.authorrondvoigts.com for updates.

About Ron D. Voigts

Ron writes murder mysteries. His sleuths have included a thirteen-year-old, a psychic, a news reporter, a playboy, a Goth witch, and a suicidal man. Researching a mystery writing class for a college extension course, he undertook to put his experience, knowledge, and skills into a five-volume series laying out easy to understand and apply methods of writing a mystery. Beyond his fiction and non-fiction writing, he creates book covers and edits work for others. Catch more about him at http://www.authorrondvoigts.com.

Made in the USA
San Bernardino, CA
31 March 2020

66629079R00044